Louis and Zélie Martin

Parents of Thérèse of Lisieux

by
Fr Paulinus Redmond

*All booklets are published thanks to the
generous support of the members of the
Catholic Truth Society*

CATHOLIC TRUTH SOCIETY
PUBLISHERS TO THE HOLY SEE

Contents

Fr Paulinus Redmond was born in Bolton and after many years as a Franciscan now lives as a solitary Hermit in Colwyn Bay. He is the author of *Louis and Zélie Martin - the Root of the the Little Flower* published by Quiller Press.

Introduction

This is a true love story. Louis Martin and Zélie Guérin fell in love at first sight. They loved all their children and wanted the best for them. Above all they loved God and desired that each of their family would also love Him.

This is also a story of battles and conflict. The Martins lived at a time of trouble for the Church and also of war between France and Prussia. Their main battle, however, was a spiritual one. Instead of bullets they used prayer which can be more powerful than atomic bombs. Prayer can move mountains! They followed the advice of St Paul and put on the armour of faith, hope and charity.

You may judge how well they achieved their ambition when you realise that one of their children is now known throughout the world as St Thérèse of Lisieux. Where necessary Thérèse will be mentioned, but this booklet is not about her. It is about Louis and Zélie and all their children who, despite set-backs and disappointments, in the end did very well. It could help you and your children to love God if you follow the example of Louis and Zélie who simply lived ordinary lives extraordinarily well.

The Families of Louis and Zélie

Paternal Grandparents

The grandparents and great-grandparents of Thérèse had a great love of God in their hearts. They lived through a time of persecution of the Church. Despite this period of persecution and repression of the Church both sides of the family kept the faith. Not only did they keep the faith, they grew in it, or rather it grew in them.

Great grandfather Jean Martin, born 1752, eventually became a captain in the French army. His son, Pierre François, was also drafted into the army. Pierre rose quickly through the ranks. Joining the 65th Heavy Infantry Regiment he soon became a corporal. Four years later he was promoted to sergeant. By the year 1813 Sergeant Martin had been promoted to second-lieutenant, and in the same year he was a lieutenant. In 1815 he became a captain. He served his country well in many campaigns throughout France and also in Belgium, Poland and Prussia. For a time he was in the 19th Light Infantry and then in the 42nd Infantry of the Line on garrison duty in Lyons.

Whilst stationed in Lyons, Pierre fell in love with Anne Boureau who was only sixteen years old. Pierre became a regular guest at Captain Boureau's home and when Anne was eighteen years old they became engaged to be married. However, the fortunes of the Boureau family at that time had suffered some reverses and so the dowry which was considered necessary for an officer's wife was lacking.

Jean Nicholas Boureau had been a gallant officer. Rising quickly through the ranks he soon became a captain. He had to retire because of ill health in 1796. He returned to the service in 1812 but was taken prisoner by the Prussians the following year. His son Jean, who was only twelve years old, was also taken prisoner and died that same year. After the Prussian campaign Captain Boureau served at Lyons where he met Pierre Martin.

On two occasions during his military career Captain Boureau was the victim of vicious false accusations which were later refuted. But by this time he had been dismissed from the army and so he could not afford a dowry for his daughter. Pierre was not going to be put off from marrying the girl he loved for lack of a dowry. What was to be done? The answer was simple. Captain Martin would provide the dowry himself!

So Anne Fannie Boureau married Pierre François Martin on 7th April 1818. They had five children. Pierre was the first, born in 1819. Then Marie Anne, born in 1820. Next came Louis, born in 1823. It was he who would be the father of Thérèse. A daughter born in 1826 was named after her mother Anne Fannie. Eventually

Anne married Adolphe Leriche. From this couple there may still be some living descendants.

The last of the five children was Sophie whom Louis loved more than the others. In fact he was her godfather. Sadly, and to the great distress of Louis, Sophie lived only nine years. In fact neither of the two brothers of Louis nor his other sister reached their thirtieth birthday.

Grandfather Pierre lived on until 1865, and grandmother Anne Fannie who was much younger survived until 1883.

As a captain in the army Pierre found that he had to move from posting to posting. Louis was born 22nd August 1823 in Bordeaux where his father was garrisoned. Unfortunately at that time Captain Martin had been called away to serve in a campaign in Spain. So Louis was privately baptised immediately after his birth and the full ceremonies of the Church were postponed until October when Captain Martin returned from Spain. The Baptismal Certificate says:

In the year 1823, on the twenty-eighth of October, Louis Joseph Aloys Stanislaus Martin, born on the twenty-third of the month of August last, lawful son of Pierre François Martin, Captain in the 19th Light Infantry, and of Marie Anne Fannie Boureau, his wife; residing at No 3 Rue Servandoni, was baptised by me, the undersigned priest. As godfather he had Léonce de

Lamothe and as godmother, Ernestine Beyssac. Signed. Jean Antoine Martegoute.

There is a slight mistake in the baptismal certificate which states that Louis was born 23rd August when in fact he was born on 22nd August.

The baptism took place in the church of St. Eulalie where there is today a monument commemorating Louis. It so happened that the Archbishop of Bordeaux, Monseigneur d'Aviau de Bois de Sanzy, was also in attendance that day. Like a faint echo of the prophecy made by Simeon to Mary and Joseph at the presentation of the Child Jesus in the Temple, something inspired the Archbishop to say: 'Rejoice, this child is a child of destiny'.

Maternal Grandparents

Isidore Guérin was born 6th July 1789 at Saint Martin l'Aiguillon. Like the paternal grandfather of Thérèse Isidore was a military man and also lived through a time of persecution of the Church. As a young boy he had an exciting escapade helping his uncle, who was a priest, to hide from the Republican troops.

At that time churches were closed. Mass had to be said in secret and priests had to be hidden away. Father Guérin was concealed in his brother's house. Isidore was given the task of accompanying his uncle on some of the apostolic journeys through the countryside.

One day when the priest was in the house, soldiers came to arrest him. They began to search through the rooms. Isidore set out some of his toys on the top of a large kneading trough and then sat down on the lid of the trough and played with toys at his side. Seeing the boy enjoying himself the soldiers passed by and continued their search from cellar to attic. Not finding the priest they went to seek him elsewhere.

When the soldiers had gone away Isidore gathered up his toys, lifted up the lid of the trough and helped his uncle to climb out.

Coming from a military background the whole family had their own special way of dealing with soldiers be they friend or foe. At the height of the Revolution, François Bohard, who was the maternal uncle of Pierre Martin, hid the church bells from the soldiers. Presumably the bells would have been stolen and melted down to make weapons of war. The parents of Thérèse once had several invading Prussian soldiers billeted with them. More on that subject later.

Father Guérin was also able to act in a military fashion when it came to dealing with enemies of the Church. One time whilst taking the Blessed Sacrament to a dying person he was confronted by three hooligans. Perhaps if he had been alone or not on such an important journey he might have stopped to reason with these three. He might have run away. He could have stood and 'turned the other cheek' to those who wished to strike him. But he was on an important journey and he was not alone. Jesus Christ was with him; truly present in the Blessed Sacrament.

Father Guérin carefully put down the pyx containing his Divine companion on a flat stone saying: 'My God, take care of yourself here whilst I deal with these three fellows.' He hurried towards his attackers, knocked them down one by one, and threw them into a shallow pond. Whilst the three were emerging from the pond and drying themselves the priest took up his heavenly guest and went on his way to give Viaticum to a sick person.

Father Guérin was not able to escape or hide for ever. He was eventually arrested and taken to prison at Bicêtre. He was then deported to the Island of Ré where he suffered the tortures and deprivations meted out to those who refused to take the oath to the Civil Constitution. As time passed by the persecution against the Church decreased and at last Father Guérin was released from prison and served as Parish Priest at Boucé in the Orme from 1802 to 1835.

Meanwhile Isidore was growing up. He was conscripted into the army and assigned to the 96th Infantry. He fought in the battle of Wagram. Later he was transferred to another division and took part in campaigns in Spain and in the battle of Toulouse. Because of this he received the medal of Saint Hélène from Napoleon III. The fall of the Emperor brought an end to Isidore's military service. He joined the foot constabulary and some time later he moved to the mounted constabulary.

It was then that Isidore met and fell in love with Louise Jeanne Macé. Louise was about sixteen years younger than Isidore but she loved him and consented to be his bride. They were married in September 1828 in the church of Pre-en-Pail in Mayenne. They lived at first in the village of Gandelain in the parish of Saint Denis-sur-Sarthon near Alençon.

The first child in this family was Marie Louise who was born in 1829. She was later to become Sister Marie Dosithée of the Visitation nuns. Then there was Azélie, born in 1831, who eventually became the mother of Thérèse. Ten years later a son was born named after his father Isidore.

Genealogy

Many people have become interested in genealogy. They wish to know who their ancestors were. The next few paragraphs trace the family lines of Louis and Zélie back to about 1650.

The paternal grandparents were Pierre François Martin and Anne Fannie Boureau. Pierre's parents were Jean Martin born in 1752 in the town of Athis-de-l'Orne; and Marie Anne Bohard born in 1753 also in Athis. They were married in 1775.

Jean had been named after his father who married Marguerite Piel in 1744. He in turn had been named after his father, Jean Martin born in 1692 also in Athis. His wife's name was Anne who was born in 1696.

The elder Jean Martin was the son of Louis Martin born 1657 in Athis; his wife being Françoise Poulau.

The paternal grandmother Anne was the daughter of Jean Nicholas Boureau and Marguerite Nay both of whom were born in Blois in 1774. They were married in 1795.

Jean's parents were Jean Boureau and Françoise Gandon, married in 1755. This Jean's parents were Gentien Boureau born 1685 at Blois, and Anne Pelouard whom he married in 1718. Gentien's parents were Jacques Boureau and Anne Boiseau who were married in 1684.

The maternal grandfather Isidore was the son of Pierre Marie Guérin and Marguerite Elisabeth Dupont. Pierre's parents were Guillaume Guérin and Catherine Huet.

Grandmother Louise Jeanne was the daughter of Louis Macé (1778-1810), and Marie Lemarchard (1783-1829) whom he married in 1803. Louis Macé was the son of a carpenter, René Macé (1732-1807) of the town of Le Horps, whose wife was Anne Grude.

René was the son of a ploughman, Jean Macé, born 1695 whom married M. Beucher in 1712. Jean Macé was the son of Nouel Macé (1660-1715), and Jeane Macé née Bignon.

God often lays His plans very deeply. All of these ancestors were part of Divine Providence. Like a wise gardener God patiently prepared the soil into which He would plant a special seed and a special root which together would produce wonderful flowers.

Youth

Young Louis Martin

Captain Pierre Martin retired from the army in December 1830. He was living in Strasbourg but decided to move his family to Normandy and chose to settle in Alençon because he considered it a good place in which to bring up his children and have them educated. They lived first of all in the Rue des Tisons.

Pierre took care that his children were brought up in the faith he loved. He made a deep impression on the people of Alençon. Many years later a lady from Alençon visited Pierre's grandchildren in the Carmel convent in Lisieux and said: 'He won our admiration by his immaculate appearance; he looked so fine in his greatcoat, decorated with the red ribbon. What a lineage of saints you have in your family.'

In keeping with his father's wishes, Louis was assiduous in his studies especially of his native language of French. He read widely and grew to appreciate books very much. He did not have the advantage of secondary school education. Instead he began to learn the art of clock and watch making. For a while he left the family home and went to live with Louis Bohard, his father's cousin, who was a clockmaker in Rennes.

As an example of how the whole family was in the habit of referring everything to God we have a letter to Louis from his mother:

> Dear son, you are the subject of my dreams by night and the chief charm of my memories. How often I think of you when my soul, upraised to God, follows my heart's longing and soars to the foot of His throne. There I pray with all the fervour of my love that God may pour out upon all my children the happiness and peace which we need in this stormy world. Be ever humble, dear son.

Whilst Louis was living in Rennes he developed a liking for the Breton style of life. He spoke its language which was similar to, but different from, French. He was often heard heartily singing 'Le Breton Exilé' and the hymn to Brittany: 'Hail Mother of the Valiant'. He was known also to enjoy wearing the national costume of Brittany.

Young Louis studied his trade of watch and clock making very well. During his apprenticeship of five years he also continued to educate himself. He went on with his avid reading of a wide spectrum of authors as is evident from his collection of extracts. These extracts were kept in notebooks to which he gave the title Literary Fragments. They were neatly written with references and an index. Amongst the collection of classical authors there are also some prayers which must have attracted him especially those that referred to the love of nature. His own final words in this collection were: 'Glory be to God Almighty and the Blessed Virgin. May God be glorified by the whole earth.

When Pierre Martin was living in Strasbourg he had a friend who was a clock maker. This friend agreed to teach Louis. So the apprenticeship was continued in that city. Once whilst taking a break from his studies and from learning his trade Louis went on a pilgrimage to the famous monastery of St Bernard in the Alps.

For some reason or other on that pilgrimage Louis collected a small wild flower. It must have caught his eye. Perhaps it was to remind him of a happy time. It must have meant a lot to him because he preserved that flower all his life. It was found amongst his belongings when he died. It was neatly dated by him. '1843'. Little did he realise then that he would produce several of his own 'flowers'.

Young Zélie Guérin

By the time Louis had completed his apprenticeship Zélie Guérin was only a little twelve-year-old schoolgirl. Neither knew the existence of the other. Zélie was born 23rd December 1831 and was baptised the following day. The Baptismal Certificate says:

On this day, the twenty-fourth of December, of the year eighteen hundred and thirty-one, Azélie Marie

Guérin, born yesterday, in and of the lawful marriage of Isidore Guérin, Gendarme, and Louise Macé, has been baptised by me, the undersigned curate. The godfather was François Michel Septier, Brigadier of Gendarmerie; the godmother, Marie Berrier, cousin of the child, who have signed with me, as also has the father, who was present. Signed F Hubert, Curate.

Although she was named Azélie, throughout her life she was known as Zélie. Born in Saint Denis-sur-Sarthon, near Alençon, she lived all her life in that area of France. Her father had retired from the army and was now a member of the local police force. Her mother was a good woman with a strong faith but was also rather austere. Zélie was not allowed to have dolls. Perhaps that is one of the reasons Zélie was keen that all her children had many toys with which to play.

Zélie's father was strict as befitted an ex-captain of the army, but he showed kindness to his children. He was keen for them to be well brought up. Wishing to see to their education he sold the family house and land in the countryside and moved to Alençon. Zélie was then thirteen years old and she, together with her sister Marie-Louise, went to the school of the Perpetual Adoration nuns as day pupils. She was intelligent and obtained first place in some subjects.

Zélie was of a delicate constitution, nearly always ill between the ages of seven and twelve. She had long periods of incessant headaches which made her head feel heavy and filled with stabs of pain. At the same time she was emotionally hurt because she felt that she was not sufficiently loved by her mother. Later in life Zélie wrote to her brother: 'My childhood and youth were cloaked in sadness for although our mother spoiled you, she was too severe to me, as you know. Good as she was, she did not know how to act towards me, so that I suffered deeply.' On a lighter note she wrote to Isidore in November 1863 telling him that she had gone to Communion and was praying for him and that she had asked the Poor Clare Nuns in Alençon also to pray for him at the exact time that he was taking his exams for his bachelor-of-science. Isidore passed he exams and eventually opened his own Pharmacy in Lisieux.

Isidore senior did not have a large pension when he retired from the gendarmerie. He tried his hand at woodwork to earn some money. For a while his wife Louise ran a cafe, but it was not very successful. Although the family was not wealthy in this world's goods, they were enriched with a strong faith. Marie Louise felt called to the Religious Life. She thought at first of trying her vocation with the Poor Clares. In the end she found her true vocation with the Visitation nuns at Le Mans. However, for several reasons she delayed joining an Order. There was work to be done at home and she also had years of doubts and scruples and was quite ill with consumption.

In the mean time Zélie was maturing. She had received a good education and had been well trained in the faith both by the nuns and her parents. So she felt called to give her life completely to God. Being of a lively character it seemed wise to Zélie to seek to enter an active Order. She also had a sympathetic nature and so sought to join the Sisters of Charity of St Vincent de Paul. Together with her mother she went to the hospital in Alençon to see the Sisters there and seek their advice. God had other plans for her.

It was decided at the interview at the hospital that she did not have a vocation to the Religious Life. It was not easy for Zélie to accept this disappointment. Nevertheless she was able to call on her strong faith to help her to see that God was indicating another sort of work for her life. So she composed this little prayer:

Lord, since, unlike my sister, I am not worthy to be Your bride, I will enter the married state in order to fulfil Your holy will. I beg of You to give me many children and let them all be consecrated to You.

Hidden deep in God's plans and unseen as yet by the world the roots of several vocations were being strengthened.

Zélie was a very practical sort of woman. She reasoned it out that her parents would not be able to provide a dowry for her. There was no guarantee that the man she might one day marry would be wealthy. In any case at that time there was not one in particular to whom she was attracted. What should she do to prepare for her future life? She asked Our Blessed Lady to help.

The answer came in an unexpected way on the feast of the Immaculate Conception, 8th December 1851. Zélie remembered that day very clearly. She said is was as though she had heard within her the words, 'See to the making of Point d'Alençon'. Immediately taking this as a sign from on high she set out to learn the trade of making fine lace.

Throughout her life Zélie habitually placed her trust in our Blessed Mother. More than once she wrote to her brother to encourage him also to have confidence in Our Lady. So for example:

> You will see that she will protect you in a very special way and that she will promote your success in this world and give you afterwards an eternity of happiness. That which I ask you to do and that which I promise you, my dear brother, is not due to any exaggerated piety of mine, nor is it without foundation, for I have reason to have confidence in the Blessed Virgin. I have received from her favours that I alone know.

Zélie had learned the basic principles of lace making at school. To make it well, however, calls for much skill and practice. It needs patience and painstaking industry to produce this beautiful hand made product for which Alençon is famous. So, at twenty years old, Zélie went to a lace-making school to learn the secrets of this craft.

Zélie learned her trade quickly and well. She was a young intelligent lively woman. A little less than average height, she had a pretty face with a well shaped nose, dark eyes and brown hair. This, together with her pleasant demeanour, made her attractive.

Unfortunately one of her instructors began to pay her more attention than she wished. Some things in life never change! Although Zélie had not completed the full course of instruction she decided to leave and set up a business of her own, whilst also attending some of the more advanced course on offer in Alençon.

The trade of Point d'Alençon is what used to be called a 'cottage industry'. Nearly all the work is done at home. In fact it is done in several homes at once. One person will specialise in one kind of stitch and another person becomes expert in another kind of stitch. The pieces are passed from house to house until complete. In some cases several pieces have to be joined together very carefully in such a way that they appear to be one piece. As the lace is already fine, this joining requires the skill of a first-class lace-maker.

Besides all this organisation of several people to make the lace pieces, yet still attending some classes, Zélie also undertook the work of taking orders from customers, buying all the necessary materials, collecting, repairing and joining the pieces of lace, and then dealing with the sale of the goods.

As a base for this work Zélie established an office in the front room of the house where the family lived in rue Saint Blaise. Very quickly she became adept at all the different aspects of her trade, and consequently she soon prospered. Convinced that this was the work that God intended her to do she carried it out to the very best of her ability. Just like the Mysteries of the Rosary of the Blessed Virgin whose help and guidance she had sought, this work was to give her much joy, a lot of light, some sorrow, but in the end, glory.

In spite of her hard-working life Zélie still considered her first duty was to God. She carried on her religious obligations as well as taking on some things which were not of obligation such as attending Mass each day of the week.

Although Zélie was doing very well financially she was not really interested in the commercial side of the business. For several years she ceased to work as a private business and worked instead on behalf of the company of Pigache.

As the years slipped by one might ask if Zélie had begun to forget that one of the reasons for taking on the trade of lace-making was so that she would have a dowry for some possible marriage. Did she wonder if there ever would be a wedding? Would there be a man she could love? If there were such a man, who was he? Where was he? Then a strange thing happened.

Meeting

One day whilst crossing the bridge of Saint Leonard in Alençon, Zélie saw a man with a dignified appearance. She looked at him. He was tall and had a high open forehead, chestnut hair and blue eyes. Before Zélie had time even to wonder who this man was, there came to her that strange inner voice which had directed her to take up the art of Point d'Alençon. This time the voice said: 'This is he whom I have been preparing for you.' The couple passed by each other. Zélie made enquiries as to who this imposing man could be. Soon she learned that this was Louis Martin the watch and clock maker.

Louis also made his own enquiries as to the name of the attractive young woman he had seen on the bridge over the river Sarthe. His mother had by chance met Zélie when they were both attending professional classes in lace-making. Soon the couple got to know each other. It was Divine Providence that these two should meet, but how had Louis been 'prepared' for this meeting?

In many ways Zélie and Louis were alike. In others quite different. Both had a long lineage loyal to the Church, devoted to God and also hard working in their worldly affairs. Each took an apprenticeship in a fine skill. They had felt a call to the life of religion. Here they differed. Zélie was a lively character and felt called to the active life. Louis was more contemplative and was attracted to a monastic life.

In September 1845 Louis went again to the monastery of St Bernard in the Swiss Alps. He applied to join the Order of Canons Regular of St Augustine. The Prior received him kindly and saw many qualities in the young man that would be suitable for the monastic life. He asked Louis about his education. Upon finding that there was a lack of classical studies and in particular of Latin, the Prior suggested that Louis return home and complete his studies especially in Latin.

Dutifully Louis went home to Alençon where the priest, Fr Jamot of St Leonard's, helped him to study Latin. As usual Louis kept precise neatly written records of his studies and expenses for books and tutelage. He bought several books in Latin, French and Greek. He also took lessons with M Wacquerie. For some unknown reason in 1847 he gave up these studies.

Because those studies had interrupted the training in his chosen craft Louis went to Paris for about a year to complete his apprenticeship. He stayed with friends and relations and avoided the temptations of the capital city as much as possible. At last he became a master of his trade and returned to his home town. There he set up his own business with the help of a friend Mlle Felicité Baudouin. He bought a house, 15 Rue de Pont-Neuf, for his watch and clock making premises. It was a large enough house for him to have his parents also live there. He was hard working and a first-class craftsman.

The business flourished and soon Louis was able to add a jeweller's shop to his premises. His good fortune and character and good looks did attract young women to him, but none of these was the one for whom he was being prepared.

There was as much fine work to be done in making a watch as there was in making lace. His work called for silence and concentration. Although he might still have felt an inclination to the monastic or even the hermit way of life Louis was not a recluse. He was keen on the game of billiards which he often played with his friends. He loved to go out walking and had a great love of nature. He was a great swimmer. On those occasions when he was not actually in the water he was just as likely to be found sitting by the river bank engaged in his favourite recreation of fishing.

Louis settled down to a steady way of life. He had by now a well established business but was not greedy. On no account would he open his shop on Sundays. Many businesses in the town might appear to be closed but they had a side door through which customers could enter furtively. Louis did not lose out financially or spiritually. God blessed him for his fidelity to the commandment. 'Remember to keep the Sabbath day holy. Six days for drudgery, for doing all the work you have to do; when the seventh day comes, it is a day of rest, consecrated to the Lord your God.'

Louis was generous to the poor. He joined an association of friends called the Vital Romet Club which was a charitable society helping the poor. There were times when Louis liked to be alone. He bought himself a small building on the south side of Alençon. This small retreat was called the Pavilion. It had three storeys with just one room on each floor. Here he kept his fishing tackle and did his reading. There was a small garden in which he planted a few flowers and a walnut tree. Louis also hung a few holy pictures and besides them also a few phrases in his own handwriting of ideas which had impressed him.

Louis was not always alone in his Pavilion for it was here that he had meeting with others who wished to help the needy or the missions. In the garden he set up a large statue of Our Lady which one day would be given the title of La Vierge du Sourir. Our Lady of the Smile. This statue had been given to Louis by his friend Mlle Baudouin. Little did he know what a tremendous part this statue was to play in the life of his family especially for his ninth child. Ninth child? In 1857 Louis was not thinking of any child nor even of a wife or marriage.

Another year slipped by. Then on that bridge of Saint Leonard he saw Zélie. There was no inner voice telling Louis that this was the girl for him. But some words from the Song of Songs might have been appropriate:

'What a wound you have made my true love. What a wound you have made in this heart of mine. And all with one glance of an eye, all with one ringlet straying on your neck.'

Louis and Zélie had fallen in love. A wedding was announced. The engagement was short. They were married within three months of their meeting.

Marriage and Children

The parish register of Notre-Dame d'Alençon records:

On Tuesday the thirteenth of July, eighteen-fifty- eight, after publication at the sermon in the church of Notre-Dame, and in that of Monsort, of the banns of the forthcoming marriage between Louis Martin, watchmaker, residing in Alençon, in the parish of Monsort, being of age, son of Pierre François Martin, retired Captain, Knight of St Louis: and of Marie Fannie Boureau; And Zélie Marie Guérin, maker of Point d'Alençon residing in this parish of Notre-Dame, being of age, daughter of Isidore Guérin and of Louise Jeanne Macé.

No impediment or opposition having been found, and the two other publications of banns having been dispensed; the civil requirements having been fulfilled; after the ceremony of betrothal, I Parish Priest and Dean of Saint Leonard, having been delegated by M L'Abbé Jamot, Rector and Archpriest of Notre-Dame, have received their mutual consent of marriage, and imparted to them the nuptial blessing, in the presence of their relatives and friends, who have signed with me. F Hurrel, Parish Priest and Dean of Saint Leonard.

In accordance with the law the civil marriage had taken place the previous day. The wedding actually took place at midnight. This may have been a custom at that time, or it may have been so that they could have midnight Mass.

The newly-wedded couple went to live in the house where Louis had his shop. There was plenty of room for the parents of Louis to have their own apartment. Besides having the watch and clock making business and jewellery shop there was still plenty of room for Zélie to establish her lace making work.

Whilst she had been waiting for God to prepare the man she was to marry Zélie had also made her own preparations. As well as her future prospects with her lace making business she brought a dowry of 5,000 francs for Louis and a further 7,000 francs of her own savings. Louis had his house, shops and pavilion all free of debt and investments of 22,000 francs. There would come a time when things were not so good financially because of the invasion by Prussia.

Louis and Zélie loved each other very much, but for a while they did not have any children. They did however soon take into their home a boy whose mother had died and whose father found it impossible to bring up his children without help. Judging by notes made by Louis from a book about marriage under the heading 'Concerning the Sacrament of Marriage' it seems that they were trying to imitate the Holy Family insofar as the Blessed Virgin and St Joseph, though truly married, observed perpetual continence.

Louis and Zélie continued to abstain for the next ten months. That they were able to control the sexual appetite, which is so strong in most people that it often seems to control them, indicates that they were willing individually and as a couple to put God before all other things even if it called for heroic sacrifice.

The Church's correct view on marriage and sex has often been misunderstood and even at times wrongly presented. God made man and woman. He created them for each other. Jesus said:

'Have you never read how he created them, when they first came to be, created them male and female; and how he said; "A man therefore will leave his father and mother and will cling to his wife, and the two will become one flesh." And so they are no longer two, they are one flesh.'

St Paul wrote in his first epistle to the Corinthians:

'Let every man give his wife what is her due, and every woman do the same for her husband; he not she, claims right over her body, as she, not he claims right over his. Do not starve one another, unless perhaps you do so for a time by mutual consent, to have more freedom for prayer, come together again, or Satan will tempt you, weak as you are.'

A wise priest advised Louis and Zélie about the Church's teaching, probably also explaining that the Holy Family were a very special case and that Our Lady and St Joseph were very exceptional sort of people.

Within a month Zélie was pregnant.

Marie and Pauline

Marie Louise was born 22nd February 1860. At her baptism in the church of Saint Pierr-de-Monsort Louis said to the priest: 'It is the first time you have seen me here for a baptism, but it will not be the last. Both he and Zélie wished to have more children.

It seemed fitting to Zélie to pray to Our Lady especially on the feast of the Immaculate Conception, 8 December, so that they would be blessed with another child. Marie Pauline was born 7th September 1861. It had been decided that all their children would have the name Marie, but would be known by their second name, except of course for the first child named Marie.

Both girls were strong babies. That was a great blessing because in those days many children died soon after being born. However when Marie was thirteen years old she was seriously ill with typhoid fever. She had to be brought home from school where she was a boarder with Pauline.

In one of her letters to her sister-in-law Zélie wrote:

'I cannot get rid of the idea that she will die. She has an extraordinary tender heart. She has not been able to accustom herself to a boarding school.

Let us hope that God will not permit so great a trial as that we should lose this child. My husband is distraught; he will not leave the house; this morning he installed himself as nurse because I was compelled to see to my workers. It makes him ill to hear her moaning and takes away his courage. Pray for us in order that should God require such a sacrifice we may have the strength to bear it.'

Zélie and Louis were exhausted with constant nursing of Marie and attending to those things which were necessary for their work and business. Seeing no sign of recovery Louis decided to storm heaven for a cure. Zélie wrote to Pauline who had been left at boarding school so as not to catch the illness from Marie: 'Your father left early this morning to make a pilgrimage for Marie. He left fasting, and will return fasting in an effort to persuade the good God to hear his prayers. He will make the journey on foot, a distance of six leagues, returning about midnight.'

Marie recovered. Her appetite returned. That pilgrimage by Louis and the prayers of the whole family must have been well received in heaven because Marie lived until she was nearly eighty year old. There would of course be many more trials and difficult times for Louis and Zélie and their family. Nevertheless one of Zélie's letters says:

> 'When we had our children our ideas changed somewhat. From then on we lived only for them. They made all our happiness, and we would not have found it without them. Nothing any longer costs us anything; the world was no longer a burden to us. As for me, my children were my great compensation, so that I wished to have many more in order to bring them up for Heaven.'

Léonie

Soon there was a blonde baby to be a new sister to the two brunettes. Marie Léonie was born 3rd June 1863. Léonie was to prove to be a difficult child to bring up although as it turned out later much of the problem stemmed from the fact that she was misled by one of the servant girls who had an overpowering influence on her. From her point of view life was difficult, and she struggled to find what she felt God was calling her to do. As a baby Léonie had not been as strong as Marie or Pauline.

In March 1864 Zélie wrote to her brother Isidore:

'Little Léonie is over nine months old and not nearly so steady on her feet as Marie was at three months. The poor child is very delicate. She has a sort of chronic whooping cough, happily less violent than that which attacked Pauline, since she would not have got over it, and the good God gives her only as much as she can bear.'

As she grew up Léonie and Zélie had many trials and misunderstandings. At the same time Zélie recognised some very good qualities in her third daughter which she hoped and prayed would some day blossom. Léonie had a kind heart and was very honest. She loved her sisters, and they loved her. Léonie did progress but it always seemed to be through a series of fresh starts. Zélie wrote to her brother:

'This poor child makes me very anxious, for her character is undisciplined and her intelligence under-developed. I cannot analyse her character; moreover the most learned would be at their wits' end. I hope all the same, that some day the good seed will spring up. If I see that, I shall sing my Nunc Dimittis.'

It was thought that Zélie's sister in the convent at Le Mans might be of help. So Léonie was sent there as a boarder. Her aunt was optimistic and gave this report:

'She is a difficult child to train, and her childhood will not show any attractiveness, but I believe that eventually she will be as good as her sisters. She has a heart of gold, her intelligence is not yet developed, and she is behind-hand for her age. Nevertheless she does not lack capabilities, and I find that she has good judgement and also remarkable strength of character. In short she is strong and generous, quite to my taste. But if the grace of God were not there, what would become of her?'

What indeed? The experiment as a boarder did not work out and Léonie returned home. They tried again in 1874 but it only lasted three months. Zélie wrote to her sister-in-law:

'My one hope in reforming this child lay in my sister. But it was necessary to separate her from other children. As soon as she is with companions she seems to lose control of herself, and you never saw anything like her unruliness. I no longer have hope of changing her nature save by a miracle. It is true I do not deserve a miracle, but I am hoping against hope. The more difficult she seems, the more I am persuaded that God will not let her remain like this. I will pray so hard that he will grant my petition. At eighteen months she was cured of a malady from which she should have died; why did God save her from death if He had not merciful designs for her?'

Many years would pass before those designs of God came to fruition. Meanwhile Léonie went to the local school in Alençon.

Hélène

Marie Hélène was born 13th October 1864. The Martins had hoped for a son, but they would have to wait a little longer for that to happen. Zélie was not well at this time and found it necessary to find a nurse for Hélène. Louis insisted that whoever the nurse might be she must be a person of good moral character. Mme Taille, known affectionately as 'Little Rose' and who lived on a farm at Semallé some kilometres from Alençon was an excellent choice.

Louis and Zélie were delighted with their new daughter. Business was going well. Léonie had been cured from a very serious disease. Zélie was beginning to feel the effects of a sickness growing within her, but she had coped with sickness more or less all her life. They hoped and prayed to have a son. Maybe he would become a priest. They would have been glad to offer such a son to God as a missionary. They would not have believed it if they had been told that one day a daughter, rather than a son, would be declared as the patron saint of the missions!

Two Sons

Marie Joseph Louis was born 20th September 1866. His parents were full of joy. Zélie wrote to her brother:

> 'It is a lovely boy, so big and strong. I could not wish for a finer child. Excepting for Marie, I never had one born so easily. If you knew how I love him. My darling little Joseph. I think my fortune is made.'

Because of her poor health Zélie again let her child be nursed by Mme Taille. New Year's day 1867 was a happy one for the family. Little baby Joseph was brought home. His mother dressed him like a prince. His four sisters delighted to hold him and kiss him. His father was justly proud at seeing his first born son. The day came to an end and Joseph was returned to his nursery at the farm.

At three o'clock in the morning the next day there was a loud knock at the door. Louis and Zélie got up to see what the matter was. 'Come quickly.' they were told. 'Your boy is very ill. They are afraid he will die.' It was an intensely cold night. In spite of the snow and slippery frost they hurried as fast as they could to Semallé.

The sickness was diagnosed as erysipelas or cellulitis. This is a skin infection in which a red, swollen area appears and spreads. The temperature rises and the person feels feverish. Joseph seemed for a while to respond to treatment but the bacteria must have got into his bloodstream. On 14th February 1867 he died.

Joseph's parents and sisters grieved at this great loss. All their hopes for him had gone. This was truly a deep sorrow for them all. Nevertheless it did not shake their faith. On the contrary it strengthened it. Joseph had been baptised. Original sin had been wiped from his soul. He was far too young to have committed any sins of his own. His body was dead, but his soul was alive and filled with the supernatural life of grace. He must have gone straight to heaven. These were the sort of thoughts that went through the mind of Zélie and Louis.

Zélie's sister wrote from Le Mans:

'Dear little sister, I received your telegram yesterday. Our little angel was then already in Heaven. How shall I comfort you? I greatly need comforting myself. I am shaking, but for all, quite resigned to God's will. Whilst praying to Our Lord this morning at Holy Communion I seemed to hear interiorly that He wished to have the first fruits, and would give you another child who would be such as we desire.'

Many years later Thérèse said that she would spend her time in heaven doing good on earth. Her brother had got there before her, indeed even before she was born. His mother soon found something for him to do. Very shortly before Joseph died Hélène had an attack of otitis. Her ear was infected and pus formed inside it. This disease makes the ear inflamed and gives a feeling of fullness in the ear, accompanied by severe stabbing pains that may prevent sleep. Hélène's ear did not respond to treatment by the doctors. Zélie got Hélène to say a prayer to her little brother. The next morning the ear was perfectly healed, the discharge had stopped all at once and Hélène felt no pain in her ear after that. Zélie obtained several other graces in this manner although not as obvious as this one.

The Martins had lost their first son. Would God grant them the grace of a second one? A novena was made to St Joseph ending on his feast day 19th March 1867. Marie Joseph Jean-Baptiste was born 19th December. The boy seemed to be strong and lively but the birth was troublesome. Zélie suffered more with this birth than any of the others, and the child was nearly asphyxiated so that the doctor, fearing the worst, baptised him.

The family friend, 'Little Rose' was called upon again to nurse the new baby. For a few weeks there was hope for the boy. Although Zélie carried on with her lace-making business she went very early each morning and again in the evening to see her son. There were weeks and weeks of bronchitis so that Joseph became exhausted with coughing. The summer weather brought a respite and Joseph was brought home but there was to be no recovery. Zélie wrote to her brother:

'I am really discouraged. I no longer feel even the strength to nurse him. It breaks my heart to see a baby suffer like him. He only utters a pitiful wail. He has not closed his eyes for forty-eight hours and he is doubled up with the violence of the pain.'

Joseph closed his eyes for the last time on 24th August 1868. His pains were over, but his parents had to suffer the loss of a second son. Undoubted they still hoped for yet one more. Zélie's sister began a friendly banter about not invoking the help of St Joseph. It looked as though the 'Saint of a Happy Death' was intent on seeing children produced only to get them into heaven as soon as possible. Zélie still insisted that the next boy would be named Joseph.

Training Children

The year 1869 was a happier time for the Martins than 1868. Celine was born 28th April 1869. She had fair hair and blue eyes. Marie made her First Communion in July. Zélie's sister who was then know as Sister Dosithée recovered her health at the convent in Le Mans. Zélie wrote to her: 'For the moment I have everything except trouble.' Zélie and Louis continued their daily attendance at Mass even though they had many customers to serve in their various trades.

Marie appeared to be shy and reserved, but underneath this timidity could be discerned a heart of gold. Pauline was a gracious and thoughtful girl. Her teachers saw potential of great talent in her. Although it was beginning to look as though Léonie would not be as bright as the others, she was behaving herself. Hélène was enchanting and quite a chatter-box.

Zélie took an active part in her daughters' education. She saw to it that they always said morning and evening prayers and taught them a formula for a morning offering:

> My God, I give you my heart; please accept
> it so that no creature, but You alone,
> my good Jesus, may possess it.

The children were taught to obey because of love, and to please our Lord Jesus Christ. They were shown how to make small sacrifices for Him. Here we can see the roots of what Thérèse eventually called her 'Little Way'. Very few of us are called to make great big sacrifices such as martyrdom, but we can all make very many little sacrifices.

Remembering how her own mother had been too strict to her, Zélie was careful not to be too demanding. At the same time she was wise enough to know that a reasonable amount of discipline is a good thing. One time when Zélie's brother was upset because his daughter Jeanne had shown her temper, Zélie told him not to be uneasy about it. Pauline had been the same when very young, but now was very well behaved. 'I must tell you, however,' she concludes in her letter, 'I did not spoil her. Little as she was, I let her get away with nothing, without making a martyr of her. But she had to give in.'

There developed in the Martin family a saying of 'setting pearls in your crown'. This was a neat way of expressing the idea that small sacrifices on earth would count as great rewards in heaven which would be seen to be like jewels in a crown. Zélie put her efforts into this training so that the words of St Peter could be said to all her children: 'When the Chief Shepherd appears you will be given the crown of glory.'

One morning Zélie took her eldest daughter to the dentist. Marie who was only nine years old was not looking forward to the visit but decided to earn another 'pearl' by offering any pain as a prayer for her recently departed grandfather. The dentist remarked that he had never seen a child so undaunted before, but decided that a bad milk tooth did not need to be taken out. Marie said to her mother when they got outside: 'What a pity. Grandfather would not have been in Purgatory.'

God is merciful and kind. He would surely have accepted the offer of that sacrifice from Marie even though she suffered no pain.

Hélène dies

The year 1870 soon brought tragedy to the family. Towards the end of February Hélène had been taken ill. At first the doctor did not think it was serious but a few days later he diagnosed a fever and choked up lungs. Hélène was to be given only broth or maybe some vermicelli or semolina, but Hélène was unable to take the broth. Zélie sat up all night with her seriously ill daughter. Hélène saw the bottle of medicine which the doctor had ordered and wanted to drink it saying that when it was all drunk she would be better. Then at about a quarter to ten she said: 'Yes, I shall soon be well again..., yes, very soon' At that moment her head fell on her mother's shoulder and five minutes later she was dead.

Louis and Zélie grieved at the loss of their young daughter. Zélie wrote to her sister-in-law: 'Sometimes I imagine myself slipping away very gently, like my little Hélène. However, those who remain need me, and for their sakes I pray God to leave me a few more years longer on earth. I feel deeply the loss of my two little boys, but I have suffered still more at losing this child. Well she is in Heaven, far happier than here below, but for me it seems as though all happiness has flown.'

Melanie Thérèse

Zélie's spirits soon picked up when she discovered that she was expecting another child. Marie Melanie Thérèse was born 16th August 1870. Zélie was determined to nurse this child herself but things did not go well. Louis did his best to find a suitable nurse but the first one did not look after Melanie well. Another was confined to bed and Melanie became ill.

Zélie tried to nurse her again and the baby looked much better and put on some weight. Her health fluctuated day by day. At the beginning of the week Melanie took to being fed. Wednesday was however a bad day. Thursday was good and the child laughed as she had never laughed before. But on Friday it was obvious she was dying. The next day, 8th October, Zélie wrote to her sister-in-law:

> 'My little Thérèse is dead, today, at one o'clock in the afternoon. At each new bereavement it seems that I love the one I have lost more than all the others.'

About the same time Zélie wrote to her brother:

> 'I wish however that the good God will give me another. I do not desire a little boy, but another Thérèse. More than two years would pass before her wish was granted.

Trouble in Rome

In 1870 there was great trouble for the Church. Many years later Celine wrote about her parents:

'Into their prayers entered the great intentions of the Church and the Holy Father. It was with sadness that we often heard of the misfortunes of the Church and of the virtual imprisonment of the Roman Pontiff.'

What was it that bothered the Martins? It is difficult for us now to grasp the anguish of Catholics in the early 1870s. For hundreds of years the Papal States stretched out over much of Europe. The Church had great influence over many worldly events. Gradually the Papal States were reduced. Pope Pius IX took refuge at Gaeta in the Kingdom of Naples for two years. By 1860 the Church's temporal power was only in the city of Rome and its surrounding districts. Italy was becoming a united country mainly led by the Piedmontese in the north. Rome was protected by French troops.

Despite all this turmoil the Pope carried out some very important work for the Church as for example the declaration of the doctrine concerning the Immaculate Conception. This was declared a dogma of the faith on 8th December 1854. Then the Pope called the first

Vatican Council in 1869. This Council went well for a while. Unfortunately the French troops were recalled from Rome because of the war with Prussia.

The Piedmontese army led by General Raffaele Cadorna attacked Rome. As soon as the soldiers broke through the city gates, Pius IX ordered his troops to cease fire. That was 20th September 1870. The Pope retreated into the Vatican and never stepped outside again. It looked as though the Church was collapsing. She had lost all her lands in Europe and the Pope had lost his freedom. The Martins, and all Catholics, had much for which to pray.

Franco Prussian War

On 19th July 1870 hostilities broke out between the French and Prussian armies. The French military leaders were Marshals Mac-Mahon and Bazaine, and Generals Bourbaki and Ladmirault. The Emperor Napoleon III was confident of victory. Man for man the French soldier was as good as the German. They also had better rifles as well as the new mitrailleuse machine gun. But they were not well led. Napoleon himself was ill. What counted most was that they were out-gunned by the German cannons manufactured by Krupp.

The war soon went badly for the French. The Ministry of War admitted that 26,000 were killed, 8,000 wounded and 50,000 captured by the enemy at Forbach and at

Worth. By mid August Sedan and Metz were besieged.
If they fell there would be nothing to stop the Prussian
advance on Paris. Marshal Mac-Mahon was wounded at
Sedan. The Emperor went to join his troops there. The
army was a strange mixture judging by its uniforms.
The blue-coated Moblots, the red of the Soldiers of the
Line. The helmeted dragoons contrasted with the long
Arab cloaks of Spahis from Algeria. The light infantry,
the Zuaves, fought gallantly. Bravely they charged at
Mars-la-Tour. But they were repelled. The ridge of
Gravelotte was taken by the Prussians and the heavy
guns pounded Metz. The Germans swept westwards
through Metz and Nancy and on to Sedan. There the
French were quickly surrounded.

Napoleon rode around under enemy fire hoping to die,
but as he saw more and more soldiers killed he
surrendered. The French elsewhere decided to fight on.
The siege of Paris began 19th September. Within days the
heights around the city had been captured. Heavy guns
pounded the forts. Brave men working for the post office
sent messages by balloon right over enemy lines. Inside
the city there was a shortage of food.

Everywhere else in France there was fear. The
euphoria of an early victory for France had been replaced
by the news that things were going very badly. The
Martins were troubled because the enemy soldiers were
now approaching Le Mans where Marie and Pauline were

at boarding school. The sound of guns could be heard also near Alençon.

Towards the end of November the people of Alençon were alarmed. They expected the Prussians any day. Half the people fled away. Zélie considered running away with Léonie and Celine, but decided to stay. As the daughter of a military officer courage came to her instinctively and she was disgusted by cowardice. Louis was too old for military service but he went out at night into the forest as a scout to observe and report on enemy movements.

Despite the obvious dangers and difficulties Louis and Zélie decided to go and bring Marie and Pauline home. They saw sadness and desolation everywhere. Zélie's sister told her that all the convents were looking after sick and dying soldiers. Many suffered from dysentry. Smallpox raged throughout the populace. Meanwhile Paris was still being bombarded.

Alençon Occupied

Colonel Lipouski attempted to hold the line at Alençon. He arrived on 14th January 1871 with 2,000 men, eight mountain guns and a squadron of Chasseurs. He was assisted by 4,000 Mobiles who had retreated at Beaumont across the bridge which he now intended to destroy. The battle commenced at half-past eleven on the morning of 16th January, less than a mile from Alençon. For a while things went well for the French. Following the gallantry shown by Captain Ducamp several companies rushed to the front and repelled the enemy. But the Prussians rallied and brought up their heavy artillery. They were also receiving reinforcements. Colonel Lipouski considered it advisable to retreat to Mezidon.

Zélie wrote about what happened next:

'About three o'clock on Monday every door was marked with a certain number of enemy soldiers to be billeted there. A tall sergeant came and demanded to see over our house. I took him up to the first floor and told him we had four children. Finally he assigned us nine.'

A huge sum of money was demanded from the inhabitants of Alençon which they at first refused to pay. They were threatened with reprisals and so they paid 300,000 francs and an enormous quantity of material. All the cattle were seized. Zélie wrote:

'Now there is no milk. What will Celine do, she drank a litre a day? And how are mothers with infants to manage? There is no more meat in the butcher's; the town is stripped. Everyone is weeping except myself.'

Zélie said she did not weep. This was not because she did not care. She was deeply moved by at the sight of so much death and destruction. How could she not be upset at having her house occupied by enemy troops? What about business? Who was interested in lace or clocks and watches when they were short of food? What about her four daughters?

To Louis and Zélie this war was a chastisement from God. What was required was not so much tears but a contrite heart. Above all what was needed was prayer. Prayer for themselves and their family and friends. Prayer for France. Prayer even for the Prussians. Louis sent in an official complaint about a soldier stealing a watch from his shop. The next day when Louis heard that another soldier had been court-martialled and shot for stealing eggs, he withdrew his complaint and pleaded for the man's life. Zélie noticed that one of the nine soldiers billeted with her was particularly sad and homesick for his family. She spoke to him and secretly gave his some extra delicacies for which he was extremely thankful. Although these men were enemy soldiers the Martins recalled that Jesus said: 'Love your enemies, do good to those who hate you. Pray for those who persecute and insult you so that you may be true sons of your father in heaven.'

That the Martins had the right attitude to this war can be judged by what happened at Pontmain. The Prussians were approaching Laval to the west of Alençon. In the nearby village of Pontmain some children had a vision of what they described as a Lady inside a blue oval frame surrounded by stars. On a banner under the vision was written: 'Pray, children, God will hear you soon. My Son will show mercy.'

This vision took place on 17th January 1871. Ten days later the armistice was signed and the Prussians moved away. Peace returned but there was a price to pay. Alsace and Lorraine would become party of the German empire. There was an indemnity of five thousand million francs. Such a huge sum of money taken out of the country put an added pressure on everyone. Louis had to sell his jewellery business and concentrate on helping Zélie with her lace-making enterprise. They moved into a house on the rue Saint Blaise.

Post-War

Louis and Zélie took up residence at 36 rue Saint Blaise in July 1871. This was to be the family home until 1877. The main entrance of the house opened out straight onto the street; there being no garden at the front. The ground floor had two large windows with exterior shutters. The first floor had three French windows topped by elegant fanlights. These windows opened on to a single long narrow balcony with iron railings. In the centre of the roof there was a dormer window.

Inside was a hallway with a door which led into the front room. It was here that Zélie did her work making lace and also attending to her lace workers when they brought in their work. The dining room was at the rear.

On the first floor there were two rooms at the front and another at the back over the kitchen. On the top floor there was a room for the younger children and another for a maid. At the rear of the house there was a garden in which Louis put up a swing for the young children. Zélie would have liked a larger garden but a laundry annex had been built which took up part of the space. Nevertheless there were many flowers and some fruit trees and a trellised vine.

France was beginning to recover from the effects of war against Prussia and also of the effects of a civil war which had been fought mostly in and around Paris. Because of these troubles Louis had lost some of his investments. Having sold his shop Louis turned his hand to caring for the financial side of the lace-making business. Zélie was pleasantly surprised as to how well he took to this new task.

The Martins were satisfied with what they had and were generous to those less well off. Celine wrote of these times many years later:

'Papa made an excellent businessman, yet with great detachment and without seeking to amass a fortune. I can see in my mind yet the place on the street where he said to me: "I feel I could easily acquire a taste for investing, but I do not want to be carried away by that current. It is such a dangerous incline and leads to speculating,'' He took the advice of Our Lord who said: 'Watch and be on your guard against avarice of any kind, for a man's life is not made secure by what he owns, even when he has more than he needs.'

Louis and Zélie worked hard so that they could afford to send Marie and Pauline to boarding school at the convent in Le Mans. Neither of the girls was keen to be away and they looked forward to the long holidays. Marie in particular did not like being at the convent. It did not enter her head that she would spend many years willingly living inside one.

Françoise Thérèse

In July 1872 Zélie wrote to her brother and his wife that she was expecting another child due about the end of the year. Marie Françoise Thérèse was born 2nd January 1873. As has happened with countless babies before and after that time, Thérèse was the cause of several sleepless nights for Louis and Zélie.

Zélie wished to feed her new child herself but the effects of an accident in her youth were beginning to show. One of her breasts was sore and did not produce sufficient milk. Thérèse became very ill. Rose Taille was asked to come from Semallé to act as nurse. Thérèse, who at one point seemed to be on the point of death, suddenly recovered. The Martins wanted Rose to stay with them, but as this was not possible it was decided that Thérèse could be taken to Semallé to be cared for there for a while. A year later the Martins were happy to see that all five daughters were in good health.

The five girls may have been in good health, but they were by no means always well behaved. Zélie wrote about Thérèse:

'As for the little ferret, I do not know what she will turn out to be; she is so little, so thoughtless, she has an intelligence superior to Celine's, but she is less gentle and has an almost invincible stubbornness.' On other occasions Zélie described Thérèse as an 'imp'.

There were many occasions when the adjective 'imp' was suitable for describing the character and actions of Thérèse. Some people might have used stronger words when Thérèse in going up to bed called out on each step and would not go on to the next until someone had replied. Unwittingly she was making the Martins exercise the gift of patience.

As had happened with the older children, Celine and Thérèse were taught to make 'jewels' for their 'heavenly 'crown' by offering little sacrifices for love of Jesus.

Life at Alençon for the Martins was certainly not all church, prayers and pilgrimages. Nor was it all work and toil. As well as the usual Sunday afternoon walks there was plenty of time given to games in the house or in the garden. All the children had several toys, and Louis would play draughts and marbles or other games with them. For himself he liked to improve his game of billiards or go fishing. They were all keen on reading.

There were also holidays away from Alençon. Zélie often took some of the children to Lisieux to see her brother and his wife and children. From there they would go on to the seaside at Trouville. Louis had a good voice and so it was a pleasure to hear him sing.

Lourdes Pilgrimage

Louis often went on pilgrimages. Zélie was not keen on travelling, but she was persuaded that she should go to Lourdes to seek a cure. She wrote:

'Really I depend now only on the help of our Blessed Mother. I am not, however, convinced that she will cure me, for it is quite possible that such is not the will of God. Everything has been done; let us leave the rest in the hands of Providence. If I am not cured it means God is holding firm and He wants me.'

Zélie was more concerned about other people's illness than her own. Thérèse had frequent colds and breathing problems. Sister Dosithée in Le Mans had consumption. Nevertheless Zélie was convinced that everything that God allows is for the best. All things, including her life or death, could be submitted to the Divine will. She could be said to have followed the advice which St Peter wrote in his first epistle:

'Bow down, then, before the power of God now, and He will raise you up on the appointed day; unload all your worries on to Him, since He is looking after you.'

On Monday 18th June 1877 Zélie, together with Marie, Pauline and Léonie, caught the train from Angers at 7.30 in the morning. Louis stayed at home to look after the younger children. Shortly before setting off Zélie wrote to her brother: 'Last night especially, I suffered very much for two hours. It is o longer possible for me to touch the sore spot. I should not be surprised if it broke open before I start. ' She also wrote:

> 'Let us surrender ourselves to God's goodness and His mercy. He will settle everything for the best. I am relying on the pilgrimage to Lourdes, but if I am not cured I shall sing the hymns just the same on the return journey.'

Zélie was always of a delicate constitution although she made up for it with her unbounded energy. In her youth she struck herself a severe blow on the corner of a table. She seemed to recover from this but in 1865 she noticed a swelling on her breast. There was no trouble for a while. Eleven years later it suddenly became clear that there was a cancerous tumour causing a great deal of pain, but which had gone too far for an operation.

Celine was allowed to see the sore on her mother's breast. She describes that moment:

> 'As to myself, I was only eight years old when my mother, at my request, showed me the sore; I have always kept an unforgettable memory of it. All the upper part of the right side of her breast as far as the shoulder and the base of the neck was bright red with inflammation, while darker red streaks ran through it, up and down.'

The journey to Lourdes was not pleasant. Marie got dirt in her eye which troubled her for hours. Léonie cried because her feet became swollen and her shoes pinched. There were other mishaps so that Zélie was worn out by the time they arrived. After sorting out the accommodation and seeing that the children were fed, Zélie went straight to the grotto. After Mass she went on to the baths. The sight of the icy cold water and the deathly cold marble around the baths made her afraid. She plunged in. The shock of the chilly water almost took her breath away. 'I should have taken things more quietly,' she admitted later.

The pilgrims stayed nearly a week in Lourdes. More trials had to be endured. Marie lost the rosary beads which had belonged to her aunt. Zélie tore her dress. Worst of all she missed a step and, in stumbling, jarred herself and twisted her neck which then gave a lot of pain. Four times Zélie went to the baths.

Those still at home were hoping for a telegram to tell them of a cure. On the final visit to the baths Zélie felt no pain as she was immersed in the water, but as soon as she came out the sharp twinges of pain returned as usual. There would be no telegram. There was no cure. But Zélie sang the hymns on the return journey just the same.

Zélie Dies

Louis took Celine and Thérèse to the station to meet the returning pilgrims. He looked and felt sad, but was pleasantly surprised to see how cheerful and contented his wife was. Almost as though she had obtained the desired miracle.

'There are great graces concealed beneath this,' Zélie said, 'and those will amply compensate me for the discomforts. The Blessed Virgin has said to us as she did to Bernadette: "I do not promise to make you happy in this world, but in the next."'

Pauline still had some time to spend at school in Le Mans disappointed at the lack of a miracle. Zélie wished to lift her daughter's spirit and to raise her thoughts to higher things and so wrote to her:

'Do not hope for many joys here below, otherwise you will have too many disappointments. For myself, I know by experience what to think of earthly joys. If I did not hope for the joys in Heaven, I should be very unhappy. Pray with confidence to the Mother of Mercies; she will come to our help with the goodness and sweetness of the most tender of mothers.'

Zélie tried her best to go to early morning Mass as she had done for years but found that she could hardly sit down or kneel without severe pain. The disease became worse day by day. She could not dress or undress herself. The arm on the sore side became practically paralysed. She could not stand upright. Her temperature rose and she felt sore all over.

By the middle of July Zélie felt sure she had not long to live. She wrote:

'It is absolutely necessary for me not to lose the little time that I now have to live. These are days of salvation for me which will never return again, and I wish to profit by them.'

Willingly would Zélie have lived on in order to help her family. At the same time her thoughts often turned to what she called, 'the homeland'. Being pulled in two directions at once was similar to how St Paul described the same feeling when he wrote to the Philippians; 'I am caught in this dilemma; I want to be gone and be with Christ, which would be very much the better, but for me to stay alive in this body is a more urgent need for your sake.'

Zélie could not settle anywhere. Sleep was almost impossible. She could not find a comfortable position for her head. When she fell asleep, the slightest movement or noise woke her and the pain began again. The cancer was spreading. Despite all this, Zélie made yet one more attempt to go to Mass on 26th July. She admitted afterwards that if there had been no-one with her she would not have had the strength to push open the door.

A few days later Zélie again said she wanted to go to Mass because her neck was not so sore, but Marie firmly and tactfully put the idea out of her mother's head. Nights were terrible for Zélie. To make sure that they did not disturb their mother the two youngest girls slept in a little bedroom over the laundry in the garden.

It was the custom at that time to wait until a person was almost at the point of death before a priest was called to administer the Last Sacraments. On Monday 27th August Louis went to get a priest and Zélie was anointed. About half an hour after midnight Zélie died.

Move to Lisieux

Louis was now a widower. He was a single parent with three teen-age daughters as well as Celine aged eight and Thérèse who was not yet five years old. What was he to do? It was suggested that the family should go and live in Lisieux. Uncle Isidore was given the task of finding a suitable home. The idea was that he and his wife, Celine, could help Louis to care for his family. The young cousins Jeanne and Marie would be companions especially for Celine and Thérèse.

Isidore looked at many house but settled eventually on one which had a large garden. On 19th September Louis went to sign the lease for 'Maison le Valois aux Bissonnets'. The five sisters took the train from Alençon to Lisieux on 15th November. They spent the night with their uncle and aunt and cousins and moved into their new home the next day. Louis stayed in Alençon for another fortnight sorting things out especially with regards to the lace-making. He arrived in Lisieux on Friday evening 30th November.

All the family liked the house except for the sound of its name so they changed it from 'Bissonnets' to 'Les Buissonnets' (The Thicket or Bushes).

Life at Les Buissonnets

It would be very easy at this point to become distracted by all the information that is available about Thérèse. Although it will be right to mention her, it is necessary to concentrate on seeing events from the point of view of her father. For example, how did he react as, one by one, his children told him of their vocations? What part did he play in that famous pilgrimage to Rome? What led him to make an offering of himself to God?

The family settled down to life in Lisieux. The two elder girls took care of the domestic affairs. A maid, Victoire Pasquier, was employed. Léonie went to the Benedictine convent school in Lisieux as a boarder. Celine went there also but as a day pupil. Thérèse was taught to write by Marie, and was given other lessons by

Pauline. Louis tended the garden. He never complained about the food even though it was obvious that Marie and Pauline were inexperienced cooks.

Léonie left boarding school in 1881 and Thérèse replaced her as a day student. Louis would often walk to school with Celine and Thérèse along the Boulevard Herbert Fournet, the Boulevard Carnot, by the Jardin Public, across the Place Saint-Pierre, down the Grand Rue, over the Pont de Caen and along the Rue de Caen.

One day as Louis was walking with his children to school Celine told him that the father of one of the girls at school had had a mental breakdown. Celine remembered this occasion because she noticed that her father shuddered and said seriously: 'That is the greatest trial a man can have.' That morning neither Louis nor his children had any idea how significant those words would become. At that moment Louis was simply intent on making sure that his children had a good Catholic education.

Even though Pauline had often talked about being a nun it still came as a shock when she said that the time had come for her to leave home. Thérèse wrote of her own feelings: 'I shed bitter tears because I did not yet understand the joy of sacrifice.' Louis did know about sacrifices. He was proud to think that his daughter had a vocation to be a Carmelite nun. He probably also thought about the part that Zélie had played and was playing. At the same time he knew that Pauline would be living in a convent from which she would not return. They would have only occasional glimpses of each other through a grille.

Louis was filled with joy which was tinged with sadness when on 2nd October 1882 Pauline entered the Carmel at Lisieux. The day for the reception of the Habit was set for Friday 6th April 1883. Henceforth Pauline would be known as Sister Agnes of Jesus.

Besides having to adjust to not having Pauline at home Louis had other things to trouble him. On 8th April his mother died at Valframbert. Thérèse became very seriously ill. The sickness and the anguish of the family went on for five weeks. Louis wept out loud as he saw that neither the doctors nor their medicine were providing a cure. He stormed heaven with his prayers. He gave Marie some gold coins to send to Paris for a novena of Masses to be said at Our Lady of Victories. The statue of Our Lady which he used to keep at his Pavilion in Alençon was placed in Thérèse's bedroom. It was this statue which to Thérèse seemed to come alive and smile as she was instantly cured of her sickness.

That summer Louis took his children on holiday for two weeks in Alençon. The years slipped by. Celine completed her studies at the Benedictine convent. Thérèse was allowed to leave school shortly after but she had to go to the home of Mme Papineau for private lessons. Léonie was still unsure of where her life was leading. On 7th October 1886 she had been accepted by the Poor Clares in Alençon and was given the postulant's habit. On 1 December she was home again.

Meanwhile Marie had confided to her father that she wished to enter Carmel and as she did so he sighed deeply and said: 'Ah, but without you...' He could not finish the sentence. He was being asked to make another sacrifice. It was on 15th October that Marie left Les Buissonets and entered Carmel.

Louis had his patience tried by Thérèse because she cried a lot. Usually for no apparent reason. When her father told her that everything was all right Thérèse stopped crying but after a few moments cried again because she had cried in the first place. This childishness continued until Christmas of 1886 when she suddenly grew up because of an incident which she describes in her autobiography.

Louis went every day to early morning Mass. He joined various Catholic associations and worked especially for the Saint Vincent de Paul Society. He still went out for walks and often went fishing. Most of his catch often ended up at the Carmelite convent. He worked in the garden and took care of the poultry and rabbits. He chopped and sawed firewood for the house. Sometimes he made cider.

At the beginning of May 1887 Louis suffered a slight paralytic stroke, but thanks to the care of his brother-in-law Isidore, he quickly recovered. On Sunday 29th May he was sitting by the well in the garden at Les

Buissonnets. The sun was going down casting a haze on the tree tops. The birds happily chanted their evening song. He could see that Thérèse had something on her mind as she sat down by his side without speaking. He must have guessed at what was coming next.

On the feast of St Joseph, 19th March, he had assisted at the ceremony for Marie's Receiving of the Habit. Afterwards he gave a dinner for the clergy at which he confided to one of them: 'I am happy; the salvation of two of my daughters is already assured. I still have one more who is only fourteen and who is already burning with the desire to follow them.'

Thérèse and Louis rose from the seat and walked for some time around the garden. Suddenly Louis spotted some little white flowers, a saxifrage, growing by a low wall. He plucked one. It came up still with its roots attached. He told Thérèse that this flower was ready to be transplanted; and so was she.

Louis did his best to help his daughter towards her true destination but there were several obstacles in the way. Uncle Isidore thought that she was much too young and should wait a few years. Canon Delatroette who was the ecclesiastical superior of the Lisieux Camel was totally opposed. Louis arranged an interview with Bishop Hugonin. Having spoken to Louis and Thérèse the bishop said he would have to consult with Canon Delatroette. Back to square one!

Thérèse enters Carmel

Louis had already booked a pilgrimage to Rome for himself, Celine and Thérèse. So it was by divine providence that an opportunity arose to seek the Pope's permission.

Louis returned from Rome with Celine and Thérèse still unsure about the outcome. Pope Leo XIII had said: 'Do what the Superiors tell you. You will enter if God wills it.' It was not until New Year's day that a letter was received from Mother Marie de Gonzague. It was good news and bad news. Bishop Hugonin had approved but the Sisters had decided that Thérèse must wait until Easter. Louis was annoyed soon afterwards when he discovered that it was Pauline who had insisted on this extra delay.

Early in January Léonie once more returned home from the convent. On the morning of 9th April 1888 Louis and his three daughters went to Mass at the Carmel convent. After Mass Louis blessed Thérèse, and the nuns led her to her cell which was roughly ten feet by seven feet with plaster walls. It contained only the essentials: a bed, a simple bookshelf, no water, no heating. The view from the window was somewhat obstructed by an adjoining wall. Thérèse loved that cell.

Louis returned with Léonie and Celine to Les Buissonnets which had many fine rooms, many books and wonderful views. But no Thérèse.

Louis makes his Offering

Louis had by now given up working in the garden. He was not as robust as he used to be. Ten years previously he had been stung behind the ear by a poisonous fly. At first there was only a small black spot. Now it had spread to the size of a hand. It was diagnosed as 'epithelioma'. It was noticed that Louis often shed tears for no apparent reason. They were tears neither of joy nor sorrow. Later he explained how he felt and what he did about it.

One day he went, as he often did, to Alençon. He usually called on friends and visited Zélie's grave. On this occasion he went to pray in the church of Notre Dame. He said that he was overcome by the goodness of God and made this prayer:

'My God, it is too much. I am too happy; it is not possible to go to Heaven this way. I wish to suffer something for You, and I offer myself.'

Besides offering himself, Louis also sent 10,000 francs to pay for a new altar at Saint Peter's in Lisieux.

Louis intended to retire in solitude and live as a hermit. In order to sort out his financial affairs he made several trips to Paris but sometimes did not return home when expected so that Léonie and Celine became worried about him. In June Louis left home without saying where he was going. Two days later he sent a letter to Celine which had been posted in Le Havre. There was no explanation at to the reason he was there. Celine went with her uncle Isidore and his friend Ernest Maudelonde to look for Louis. It took them two days to find him. It turned out that Louis had begun to suffer from arteriosclerosis which restricted the flow of blood to his brain and his legs. He began to have bouts of forgetfulness and hallucinations.

Although Celine felt called to the Carmelite life she determined to stay at home and she and Léonie looked after their father. There were good days as well as bad. Thursday 10th January was a very happy day. This was the day when Thérèse received the Carmelite Habit. Louis thoroughly enjoyed taking part in the ceremony. However, towards the end of the month he had alternate bouts of over-stimulation and drowsiness. The cerebral paralysis grew worse. His brain was impaired. He had lapses of memory. His imagination played tricks on him. He thought he was seeing frightful things, slaughter and battles. He could hear the sound of cannons and drums. When he was told about a robbery in the town he wanted to carry his revolver with him at all times to defend his home and family.

When uncle Isidore heard about all this he feared for the lives of his nieces. He asked his friend Vital Romet

who was a tall strong man to come and help him disarm
Louis. Very reluctantly it was decided that it would be
best if they took Louis to the Bon Sauveur Home at Caen
where they looked after the mentally ill.

Caen

On the way to the station to go to Caen, Isidore and his
friend took Louis for a quick visit to the Carmel convent.
Louis thought that he was going for a short trip to the
coast, but when they got to the Bon Sauveur Home he
realised where he was and why. He made no objection.
Did he recall, as Celine did later, that he had said of
someone who had a mental breakdown: 'That is the
greatest trial a man could have.'?

For a while Léonie and Celine rented a room in Caen
near the Home, but as the regulations only allowed visits
once a week, they returned to Lisieux.

Unfortunately by then several people in Lisieux were
making cruel remarks. It was said that this illness had
been caused because Louis was disturbed by his
daughters entering the convent. Especially his youngest!

The attitude to the mentally ill was in general far
worse then than it is today. People would willingly use
words such as 'crazy, lunatics, and cretins.' They would
refer to them as being in the 'loony bin' or 'madhouse'.
The understanding of the causes and also the treatment of
this illness were also much less than now. How could

Louis explain that he was delighted that his daughters were in Carmel?

Those in the convent could do nothing but pray. Léonie and Celine had to endure hearing those nasty remarks. Louis simply said: 'I had always been accustomed to commanding, and I see myself reduced to obeying; I never had any humiliations in my life, and I needed one.' The doctor to whom Louis made this remark replied: 'Well this one can count.'

Louis dies

Les Buissonnets was too large a property for the two sisters. The house was sold and Léonie and Celine went to live with the Guérins in Lisieux and sometimes also at a family home in La Musse. Meanwhile the paralysis in their father's lower limbs became worse. By Easter 1890 he could hardly stand upright.

In March 1891 Celine was very sick. Her uncle and aunt saw that she was very upset by her father's continued illness. They proposed that she should not go so frequently to see him. The doctors recommended that she should avoid any emotional upsets. Léonie and Celine therefore made few visits to Louis. There was very little they could do for him.

Celine's health began to recover but she had another problem to cope with. Henry Maudelonde, a lawyer in Caen, had fallen in love with her. Celine wrote of this later: 'I belonged to Jesus alone. I had given Him my pledge, but I found the marriage vocation beautiful also; I had, so to speak, two vocations, two attractions. I would have to speak only one word or give just one look. When I look back on it my vocation was holding on by a thread.

Léonie and Celine, hoped to be able to take their father back to Lisieux, but did not do so until the following May. Louis stayed in a bedroom on the second floor of the Guérin's home for a few weeks. Then Léonie and Celine took him to a house which faced the back garden of their uncle's house. Louis was given a room on the ground floor. He was happy as he could be. Désiré, the manservant, was tall and strong so that Louis only needed to put one arm around his neck to be lifted out of a carriage and placed in an armchair.

Although his arms were not paralysed, he could only move them partially. His legs were as though stuck lifelessly together. His mind was still affected by seizures so that he appeared to be somewhat childish. At the same time it was noticed that he often knew what was going on around him and suffered by not being able to express himself properly.

With the help of the manservant Désiré they were able to take Louis occasionally to La Musse where they could wheel him around the woods and he could see the countryside which he loved so much. In July 1895 the family took Louis again to La Musse. Things went well for three weeks, but then Louis had a prolonged heart attack. He was anointed. The following morning, Sunday 29th July 1894, as Celine was kneeling by the side of her father's bed she prayed aloud: 'Jesus, Mary, and Joseph, I give you my heart, my soul and my life. Jesus, Mary and Joseph assist me in my last agony. Jesus, Mary and Joseph may I breathe forth my soul in peace with you.' Louis opened his eyes for a moment and then closed them for the last time. The funeral took place four days later at the Cathedral of St Pierre in Lisieux.

Celine entered Carmel in Lisieux 14th September 1894, and was known as Sister Genevieve. She died there in 1959. Léonie finally entered the Visitation convent in Caen 28th January 1899. She took the name of Sister Françoise Thérèse. She died there in 1941.

The remains of Louis and Zélie have been laid to rest side by side in a special place at the back of the cathedral which was built in honour of their daughter.

Venerable

The causes of Louis and Zélie Martin were drawn up between 1957 and 1960 in two separate processes whose findings were sent to Rome.

The two causes are now being examined as one single cause so that husband and wife may be beatified together as a married couple should the Church so decide.

The material (two volumes) on the 'Position on the Heroic Virtues' of the Servants of God was presented to the Congregation for the Causes of Saints on 2nd May 1991 and consequently placed on the list of 'Positions' awaiting their turn for discussion by the Theological Consultors of the Congregation.

The outcome of this discussion was positive. The 'Position' was passed on to the Cardinals of the appropriate Dicastery and finally to the Holy Father for his approval.

The 'Decrees of the Heroic Vitues' of these two servants of God was promulgated on 26th March 1994. Louis and Zélie Martin were declared 'Venerable' as a couple by His Holiness Pope John Paul II.

Beatification

Pietro Schillero was born in Monza on 25th May 2002. His lungs were in such a terrible condition that the doctors gave little hope for his survival. Pietro was given respiratory assistance, but nobody thought that he would ever be able to breathe normally. Pietro's parents and their parish made a novena to Louis and Zélie Martin. On 29th June Pietro was much better and left the clinic on 26th July in perfect health.

On 10th June 2003, in his private chapel, the Cardinal Archbishop of Milan, Mgr. Dionigi Tettamanzi, surrounded by judges and secretaries signed the Act for the official closure of the process recognising this miraculous cure. All the Schillero family were present including thirteen month old Pietro who paraded around the chapel and even crawled under the desk where the Cardinal was signing the Act.

On Thursday 3rd July 2008 at a Private Audience with Cardinal José Saraiva Martins, C.M.F., Prefect of the Congregation for the Causes of Saints, Pope Benedict XVI authorised the promulgation of the Decree concerning a miracle attributed to the intercession of the Venerable Servants of God, Louis and Zélie Martin.

This single miracle, obtained through the joint intercession of these holy parents, was considered sufficient for the Beatification ceremony to take place at the Basilica in Lisieux on Sunday 19th October 2008. Now just one more miracle is required for the canonization of Louis and Zélie Martin.

Conclusion

Some people might think that this holy couple are being considered for canonization simply because they were the parents of St Thérèse; ignoring the fact that Thérèse achieved sanctity because she was the daughter of Louis and Zélie Martin. Others might say that they did nothing special. They were born, worked at their own trade, met, fell in love, married and had children. Nothing more than you could do. That is just the point. Instead of doing one or two outstanding things, they did very many little things very well. In other words they lived what Thérèse would describe as her 'Little Way to Heaven'. But it was not she who taught them this 'Little Way'. It was they who taught her!

The Little Way
of St Thérèse of Lisieux

Hardly twenty-four years of age, Thérèse Martin died of tuberculosis in Normandy in 1897. From a large family, her mother had died of breast cancer when Thérèse was only four. Her father, a master watchmaker, died after years in a mental hospital. These writings show how it is that this young French woman, in such a short life, has inspired millions. In recognition of her special teaching mission for God's people, the Church has proclaimed her a Doctor of the Church - the only woman apart from St Catherine of Sienna and St Teresa of Avila.

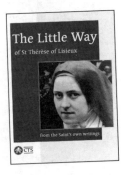

ISBN: 978 1 86082 389 7

CTS Code: D 306

Thérèse
Teacher of Prayer

St Thérèse of Lisieux has much to teach us about prayer. This delightfully simple booklet will help all those wishing to follow the young Carmelite's way of praying with the heart. In doing so, Brother Craig takes us through some of the richest traditions: Eucharistic adoration, devotion to Our Lady and veneration of the saints and angels. Above all we are reminded by Thomas a Kempis that 'Grace walks in simplicity, in doing all things purely for God'. This is what Thérèse can teach us. Prayers to and by Therese are included.

Brother Craig, founder of The Monks of Adoration and graduate of Albuquerque University, gained his S.T.L. in Theology in Rome. He has written several columns, articles, short stories, poetry and five books.

ISBN: 978 1 86082 480 7

CTS Code: D 693

Thérèse of Lisieux

Born in 1873 at Alençon in France, Marie Françoise Thérèse Martin died in 1897 aged 24 of advanced intestinal tuberculosis, at her Carmel convent in Lisieux. 100 years later John Paul II declared her a Doctor of the Church. She was canonised as a saint, in record time, only 28 years after her death. She never went to university, hardly travelled, had no academic or other titles. Yet she (through her story and writings) was almost a household name during the Great War of 1914. This authoritative life of Thérèse, a true classic, tells the story of one of Christ's true 'little ones'.

The relics of St Thérèse, which have so far visited nearly 40 countries, will be coming to England and Wales in September 2009. There will be an opportunity to venerate them at major locations. Wherever St Thérèse's relics have gone, there have

been many graces of conversion, healing and discovery of vocation. Full details, visit *www.catholicrelics.co.uk.*

ISBN: 978 1 86082 146 2

CTS Code: B 204

The Message
of St Thérèse of Lisieux

Thérèse died a painful and lingering death of tuberculosis in her French convent in the Normandy town of Lisieux in 1897, at only twenty four years of age. Thousands of soldiers in the First World War trenches carried her picture to their own deaths. This acclaimed booklet sets out what Thérèse called her *Little Way* and powerfully reveals the relevance of the Gospel to everyday living.

The relics of St Thérèse, which have so far visited nearly 40 countries, will be coming to England and Wales in September 2009. There will be an opportunity to venerate them at major locations. Wherever St Thérèse's relics have gone, there have been many graces of conversion, healing and discovery of vocation. Full details, visit *www.catholicrelics.co.uk.*

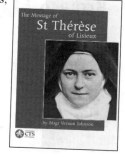

ISBN: 978 1 86082 013 7

CTS Code: D 331